ADO(RED) INSPI(RED) SHA(RED) TREASU(RED) ADO(RED)
POWE(RED) KIND(RED) ADMI(RED) CHEE(RED) ENAMO(RED) SHA
RED)IBLE SHA(RED) EMPOW(RED) ADO(RED) ADMI(RE
RED) KIND(RED) ADMI(RED) INC(RED)IBLE KIND(RED) SHA
BLE EMPOWE(RED) TREASU(RED) ADO(RED) CHEE(RED) KI
INSPI(RED) KIND(RED) ADMI(RED) CHEE(RED) ENAMO(RED
ADO(RED) INSPI(RED) SHA(RED) ADO(RED)
POWE(RED) KIND(RED) ADMI(R ENAMO(RED) SHA
RED)IBLE SHA(RED) EM ADO(RED) ADMI(RE
RED) KIND(RED) ADMI(RED) INC(RED)IBLE KIND(RED) SH
BLE EMPOWE(RED) TREASU(RED) ADO(RED) CHEE(RED) KI
INSPI(RED) KIND(RED) ADMI(RED) CHEE(RED) ENAMO(RED
ADO(RED) INSPI(RED) SHA(RED) TREASU(RED) ADO(RED)
POWE(RED) KIND(RED) ADMI(RED) CHEE(RED) ENAMO(RED) SHA
RED)IBLE SHA(RED) EMPOW(RED) ADO(RED) ADMI(RE
RED) KIND(RED) ADMI(RED) INC(RED)IBLE KIND(RED) SH
BLE EMPOWE(RED) TREASU(RED) ADO(RED) CHEE(RED) KI
INSPI(RED) KIND(RED) ADMI(RED) CHEE(RED) ENAMO(RED
ADO(RED) INSPI(RED) SHA(RED) TREASU(RED) ADO(RED)
POWE(RED) KIND(RED) ADMI(RED) CHEE(RED) ENAMO(RED) SHA
RED)IBLE SHA(RED) EMPOW(RED) ADO(RED) ADMI(RE
RED) KIND(RED) ADMI(RED) INC(RED)IBLE KIND(RED) SH
BLE EMPOWE(RED) TREASU(RED) ADO(RED) CHEE(RED) KI

D1200997

) INSPI(RED) SHA(RED) TREASU(RED) ADO(RED) INC(RED)
RED) KIND(RED) ADMI(RED) CHEE(RED) ENAMO(RED) SHA(RED
LE SHA(RED) EMPOW(RED) ADO(RED) ADMI(RED) KIND(
(RED) ADMI(RED) INC(RED)IBLE KIND(RED) SHA(RED) INS
MPOWE(RED) TREASU(RED) ADO(RED) CHEE(RED) KIND(RE
PI(RED) KIND(RED) ADMI(RED) CHEE(RED) ENAMO(RED) ADMI(
) INSPI(RED) SHA(RED) TREASU(RED) ADO(RED) INC(RED)
RED) KIND(RED) ADMI(RED) CHEE(RED) ENAMO(RED) SHA(RED
LE SHA(RED) EMPOW(RED) ADO(RED) ADMI(RED) KIND(
(RED) ADMI(RED) INC(RED)IBLE KIND(RED) SHA(RED) INS
MPOWE(RED) TREASU(RED) ADO(RED) CHEE(RED) KIND(RE
PI(RED) KIND(RED) ADMI(RED) CHEE(RED) ENAMO(RED) ADMI(
) INSPI(RED) SHA(RED) TREASU(RED) ADO(RED) INC(RED)
RED) KIND(RED) ADMI(RED) CHEE(RED) ENAMO(RED) SHA(RED
LE SHA(RED) EMPOW(RED) ADO(RED) ADMI(RED) KIND(
(RED) ADMI(RED) INC(RED)IBLE KIND(RED) SHA(RED) INS
MPOWE(RED) TREASU(RED) ADO(RED) CHEE(RED) KIND(RE
PI(RED) KIND(RED) ADMI(RED) CHEE(RED) ENAMO(RED) ADMI(
) INSPI(RED) SHA(RED) TREASU(RED) ADO(RED) INC(RED)
RED) KIND(RED) ADMI(RED) CHEE(RED) ENAMO(RED) SHA(RED
LE SHA(RED) EMPOW(RED) ADO(RED) ADMI(RED) KIND(
(RED) ADMI(RED) INC(RED)IBLE KIND(RED) SHA(RED) INS
MPOWE(RED) TREASU(RED) ADO(RED) CHEE(RED) KIND(RE

BE INSPI(RED): Words of Hope and Courage
Copyright © 2007 by Hallmark Licensing, Inc.

Published by Hallmark Books, a division of
Hallmark Cards, Inc., Kansas City, MO 64141.
Visit us on the Web at www.Hallmark.com.

All rights reserved. No part of this publication
may be reproduced, transmitted, or stored in
any form or by any means without the prior
written permission of the publisher.

Editorial Director: Todd Hafer
Art Director: Kevin Swanson
Designer: Michelle Nicolier
Production Artist: Dan Horton
Contributing Writers: Stacey Donovan,
Jim Howard, Linda Morris, Sarah Mueller,
Tina Neidlein, Dan Taylor, Melvina Young

ISBN: 978-1-59530-110-9
BOK5530

Printed and bound in China

BE INSPI(RED)

Words of Hope and Courage

BE INSPI(RED)

What is (RED)™?

(RED) is not charity; it's a business plan with a heart, a profit model with a mission.

The Global Fund is the best weapon we have against the AIDS epidemic, which kills 5,800 people in Africa alone every day. The Global Fund saves lives by funding effective, local treatment and prevention programs. Only one percent of the money given to the Global Fund came from corporations. Until (RED).

(RED) is a partnership with the world's most iconic brands to make great products and give a percentage of profits to the Global Fund. **(RED) allows anyone—you and me—to help fund AIDS relief every day.** By shopping. By making doing good profitable. And fashionable. And sustainable.

A bunch of us here at Hallmark thought the idea was brilliant. So when (RED) came calling to ask if we'd like to join in the effort, we said YES. Now when your mom has a birthday or you want to give someone a gift, like, say, a book, you can choose (RED). **We are so proud to be a part of this world-changing business model. We hope you are, too.**

To learn more about (RED), visit JOINRED.COM.

Introduction

If you ever doubt the power of language, listen more closely. Witness the magic the first time someone whispers "I love you."

Watch a woman put on headphones, close her eyes, and have her life changed by a lyric.

See a bad moment flipped upside down by a well-timed joke.

Words propel us, empower us, make us human... and more than human.

We constantly struggle to say what we mean
and mean what we say.

To "wrestle with words and meanings."
That's what T.S. Eliot calls it.

But as we whisper and shout, stutter and spin,
we create order out of the chaos around us.
We are built of words, and we live by them, too.
This book is about a few of our favorites.

Potential is nice.

Talent is wonderful.

But so few of us ever use what we have.

You can make an impact that's better than nice

and bigger than wonderful.

You can be incredible.

(red)ible

Sacred is discovering what you believe
and then believing what you discover.

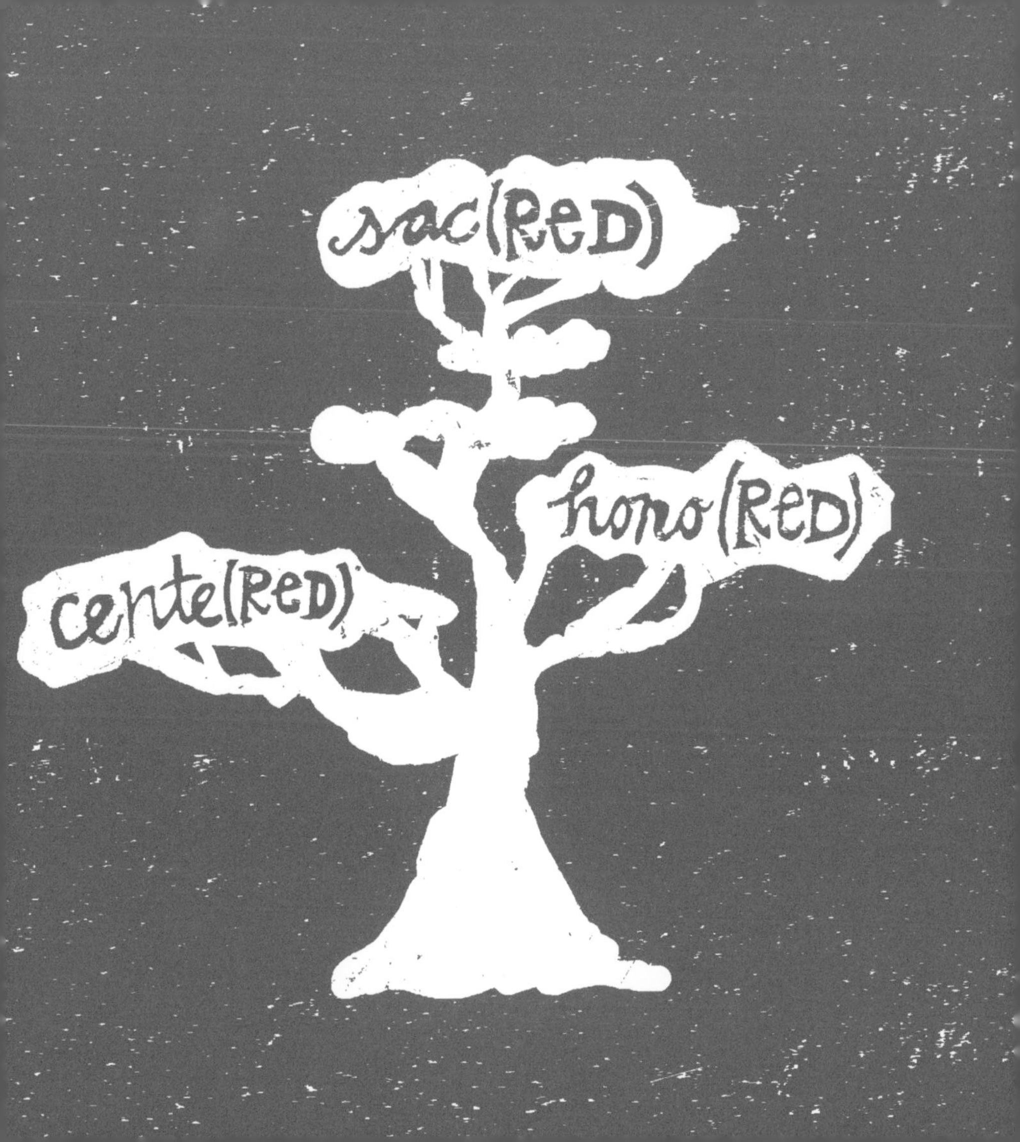
sac(RED)
hono(RED)
cente(RED)

C(RED)IBLE

Credibility.
Choose it. Protect it. Guard it. Never deny it.
Because, in the end, the truth will always come out—
and win out.

(RED)EDICATE

Even when you're grown up,
sometimes it's a good idea
to put things back
where you found them.

deciphe(red)

No one can solve everything.

But *everyone* can solve *something*.

So. Start small. Ask for all the help you can stand.

Who cares how it looks, or if every piece falls into place

right on time? Who said it was a race? Just get the wheels

under the thing and put it on the road.

Are you going in the right direction?

Yes—because you're trying. You care.

You've cracked the code.

RECONSIDE(RED)

Opinions that are set in stone are heavy.
And that's about all they have going for them.

PREPA(RED)

Write your detailed lists. Make your impeccable plans. But someday you will find yourself short of something. Wanting. Desperate, even. And the only thing that will get you through is humility. The ability to ask for help. For directions. For a second chance. Chances are, a fellow traveler will have just what you need.

A touch. A glance. A smile.

Little moments that bind us to each other

in an instant of common experience.

They change us. They fill us with memories.

Embrace them.

It's the things we share that remind us we're not alone.

sha(red)

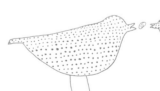

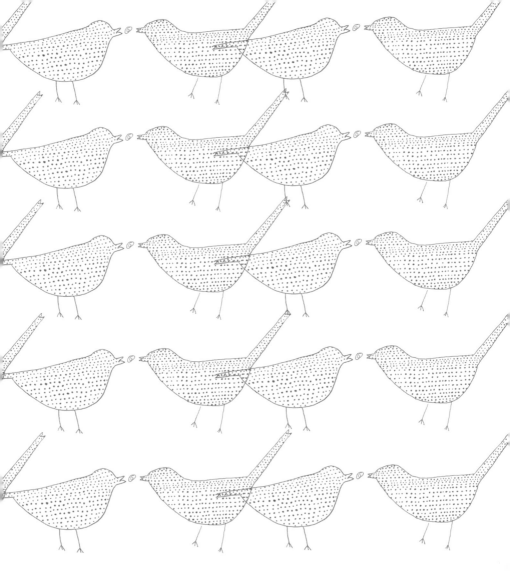

They will tell you to be realistic.

They will tell you to manage your expectations.

They will tell you to set reasonable goals.

Refuse treatment.

Remain irreconcilably, incorrigibly infected with hope,

and you will see things beyond your most impractical dreams.

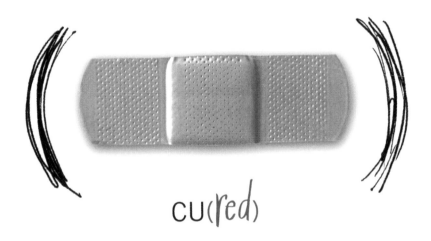

cu(red)

Dig deep. Look within. It's all there inside you.
Except sometimes…it's not.
Everybody has days when all
the digging deep only turns up mud.
And that's when you hand over the shovel.
You reach out. You let somebody give you
what you can't mine for yourself.

We are strongest together, holding hands.

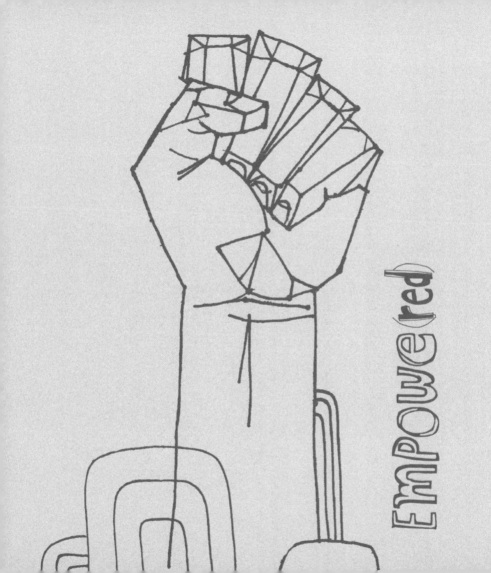

EmPOwe(red)

ASSU(RED)

If every living body
were assured of love,
peace could create itself.

WI(RED)

Sizzle with the now,
fire yourself up
and blaze beyond
the path of what could be
to ignite what is.

Every year, a tree draws a new ring around itself,
as if to say: See? There's more life in me than there used to be.
Maturity doesn't just mean you've weathered storms
or survived drought. It's about taking in more of everything:
more light, more rain, more of time's slow sweetness,
and giving something back.
If you've matured, you've expanded your circles.

matu(red)

REDISCOVE(RED)

Rediscover you.
Admire yourself more often.
You are as beautiful
as your heart remembers.

REDISCOVE(RED)

Rediscover you.
Admire yourself more often.
You are as beautiful
as your heart remembers.

HONO(RED)

Smile for a stranger.
Find the time when you have none.
A simple, human gesture inspires others
to go with the flow. Such a small gift,
such simple greatness, has moved mountains
and is inside us all.

There is love embedded in the subtle simplicity of every day.
Don't overlook its gentle magic.
It is life's gift. Take it.
Let it charm you.

desi(red)

That thing beating in the middle of your chest...
what's inside it right now?
Oh, sure, blood and arteries and stuff.
But what is deeper than that?
Have you taken a peek lately?
Get in there. Snoop around.

Get to know exactly what it is that heart of yours desires.

So you don't have a mascot. Or team colors.
Or a fight song that plays every time you enter a room.
But, wow! Do you have a following!
A support system. People who are
gonna stand by you in victory or defeat.
And they're ready to chant, "Let's get fired up!"
whenever you need it.
No matter what...never, ever forget your fans.

Chee(RED)

ASPI(RED)

Sunflowers get their name
because they turn their faces to the sun.
After a long time of doing that,
they start looking like the sun itself.
So keep looking up.
You are already becoming the person
you wish you could be.

TI(RED)

You wouldn't believe how many
amazing things happened
right before the person trying them
was about to give up entirely.
It's, like, *most* of the amazing things.
Really.

REDO

(ReD)o

Starting over is the bravest kind of starting there is.

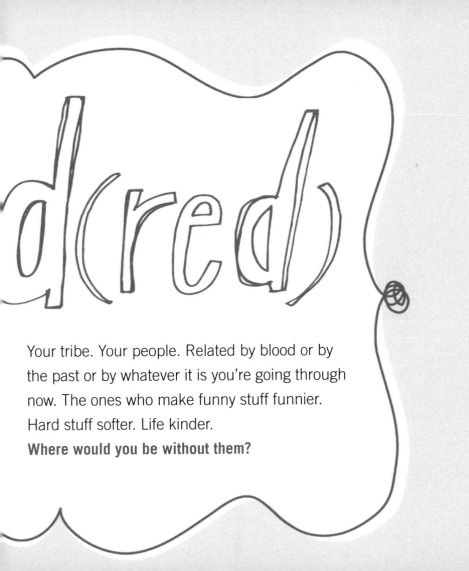

Your tribe. Your people. Related by blood or by the past or by whatever it is you're going through now. The ones who make funny stuff funnier. Hard stuff softer. Life kinder.

Where would you be without them?

REMEMBE(RED)

That's the question.

What do you want to be remembered for?

It's not really about *what* you made of your life.

It's about *how* you made your life.

How you made the world.

Maybe just a little bit better? Then you're doing fine.

C(RED)O

It's not good enough to believe in something.
It's got to be something good. Something big.
Something strong enough to get you through
the most hellish night you can fathom—
and the most beautiful morning you can imagine.
So believe in something, yes.
But, please, believe in something great.

PERSEVE(RED)

It takes a glacier about a year
to move as far as you can walk in a few minutes.
Eventually, it carves out canyons
and slaps up mountains.
It permanently changes the world.
Just by keeping at it.
So can you.

Some people just seem to make
an adventure out of everything.
Not surprisingly, those are the people
who seem to keep having adventures.

The people looking up to you are so busy looking up
that they don't often mention how much you mean to them.
They know you'll understand,
which just makes them admire you more.

Some people live their lives like each new moment
is an opportunity for discovering some great thing.
That's cool. But don't miss the opportunity to make
accidental discoveries just by sitting still. And watching.

And waiting to see what happens.

Everybody needs some taking care of.
Even if they look like they don't. Even if they look all tough
and strong, like they could survive on their own
in the wilderness for a year with nothing but a lighter.
And, yeah, even if "they" happens to be you.

So take care.

NURTU(RED)

(RED)EEM

Here's the real secret: There is nothing—
absolutely nothing—that can't be stitched up,
cleaned up, bound up, or brought back together.
With enough faith, strength, and love,
there is nothing—
and no one—beyond saving.

RESTO(RED)

It's amazing how little things can restore your faith in people.
Situations get messy sometimes and you think,
"What's the point?" Then somebody
does some cool thing for somebody else.
Just one little amazingly human thing and you realize…
there might be something to this whole "humanity" bit.

You realize…we can do this.

You open up all the windows and you can see forever.
The ideas float in and crowd out your worries, your details,
and fill you up with words and colors and wings.

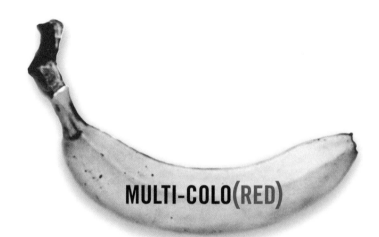

Ever notice that the colors in nature
are also in humankind?
No, there aren't orange or green
people running around.
But there are people who are the color
of sunny summer peaches and purple-black plums.
People with undertones of ripe banana
or fresh ginger in their skin.

All with red, red blood running underneath.

All beautifully human.

Speak up, will you?

Say what you really want to say for once,

not what you think people want to hear.

See how good it feels to open that gate in your head

that keeps those bold thoughts inside.

Get mouthy. Let the world hear it.

The world just might pay attention.

UNCENSO(RED)

UNP(red

ictaBLe

Okay, fine, history repeats itself.

Doesn't mean you have to.

Why not give all who think they know you

a little surprise party now and then?

Dance when you should be walking.

Speak when you should be quiet.

Do whatever it's gonna take for you to say,

"Did I really do that?"

Commit a few random acts of you-ness.

DELIVE(RED)

Maybe the true miracle of life
isn't conception or pregnancy or birth
but that deep connectedness we sometimes feel:
the invisible cord that binds us together.
Maybe the real miracle is how we're all delivered,
from one moment to the next,
into a world that needs us,
needs the gifts only we can give,
right here, right now.

ENTE(RED)

One sure way to get through a maze
is to keep one hand on the wall,
continuously, as you go.
You'll walk in and out of some dead ends,
and you might miss some shortcuts,
but all the walls of a true labyrinth are connected.
Make contact, and you're touching
the whole thing, from entrance to exit.
Just stay in touch. You'll get there.

You only live once, right?

Cause some commotion, then! Order dessert.
Go redhead. Get the motorcycle. Do something—
anything—that makes people say, "Man, you're nuts!"
Make the adventure of a lifetime life itself.
Just don't forget to wear a helmet.

DA(RED)EVIL

Meet the authors of BE INSPI(RED)— and their favorite (RED) words . . .

LINDA MORRIS: "My favorite (RED) word is savo(RED), and the reason is that it's a lingering appreciation; the passionate memory of an experience, emotion, or sensation that has touched you. If you can learn to savor and show others how to do it, then you've truly lived."

JIM HOWARD: "I like the word sca(RED) for two reasons: 1) One of the great discoveries of life is that fear is good—without it, you'd never know what courage is. And 2) if you put the 'red' into it and say it the way it looks, you're scat-singing. Sca-red-ba-dooby-scooby-zooby-wahhhh. . . . Nothing beats fear like scat-singing."

MELVINA YOUNG: "My favorite is kind(RED). I love my family and generally make 'brothers' and 'sisters' of my friends. I really believe in the power of compassion and the human capacity to do right by each other. To take care of each other in the fullest sense. As old-fashioned as it seems, I still believe in the 'family of man.'"

DAN TAYLOR: "I like the flexibility and the power of sac(RED). It's a word that represents ideas that are completely individual, but universally shared."

TINA NEIDLEIN: "The older I get, the more I strive to be uncenso(RED). There's such an amazing feeling of freedom that comes when you let your guard down and give the real you a chance to speak up. (Turns out, the real me swears way too much.)"

SARAH MUELLER: "As a distance runner, I like the word endu(RED). You need endurance to do anything in life."

STACEY DONOVAN: "I'm a fan of perseve(RED). Because I've noticed that sometimes in life good things happen just because you're too stubborn or deluded to quit."

✳

INSPI(RED)?

If you've enjoyed these words
of hope and courage,
please let us know.

SEND YOUR COMMENTS TO:

Book Feedback
Hallmark Cards, Inc.
2501 McGee, Mail Drop 215
Kansas City, MO 64108

Or e-mail us at booknotes@hallmark.com.